THE ORATOR

Wayne Haddon

© 2019 Wayne Haddon

Wayne Haddon asserts the moral right to be identified as the author of all works contained in this collection 'The Orator'.

ISBN: 978-0-6485587-2-9

All rights reserved. No part of this publication may be reproduced, stored in a retrieval system, or transmitted, in any form or by any means, electronic, mechanical, photocopying, recording or otherwise, without the prior permission of the author..

I'd like to acknowledge my dad, Paul Lewis Haddon, who is the good voice in my head and keeps me on the right path. I'd also like to thank Virginia Wall, my best friend and support, also Susan Haddon and Cecile Hunt for encouraging me along the way. A special thank you to Darren Saul, Leone Sperling and Evan Shapiro for their much valued technical work on the book.

I have known Wayne for 12+ years and greatly appreciate his poetry, art and music. Wayne bravely gives us amazing insights into his special world--sometimes baffling, dark, humorous, tragic, raw, loving or pensive...but always a significant view of this mind. Wayne has the gift of using words and concepts in an alliterative manner that gives rhythm to his lines and wonderful 'running rhyming' of consecutive words that gives poignancy and strength.

Wayne and his 'voices' give us an incredible opportunity to witness, learn and hopefully better understand his complicated journey.

I salute Wayne for sharing his thoughts art and words...Perhaps his works will help destigmatise mental issues and benefit the many who live each day with mental challenges.

Cecile Hunt
Sydney

CONTENTS

Bad news is good news 7	Lovers embrace 49
Bits 8	Lullaby 50
Daughter 9	Lust 51
Docs & leathers 10	Mad 52
Expression 11	Mention 53
Forever is never 12	Open book 54
Gear 13	Poverty 55
Haters 14	Pride 56
In the strangest places 15	So bad it's good 57
The box 16	Spaceship 58
Love 17	War 59
Money 18	What's wrong 60
No greater no lesser 19	You make my life hell 61
Now you see it now you don't ... 20	Bad rap 62
Respect 21	Dark ghost 63
Rolling thunder 22	Dishes 64
Sets 23	Drugs 65
Shades of light lyrics 24	Friends in a jam 66
Target 25	Hold 67
Prophet 26	Ladies please 68
That's how i roll 27	Lonely crowd 69
The machine 28	Man in place 70
The start 29	Resistance is futile 71
The sword 30	Rolling eagles 72
What's in the medication 31	Ruby rock city 73
Wings 32	Sensory overload 74
Addiction 33	Space junk 75
Been around 34	What's the meaning of life 76
Big time friends 35	The original 77
Cheers 36	Think on this 78
Drunken sense 37	Tunnelling in 79
Dumb dumber dumbest 38	Zen 80
Finding middle ground 39	The pop up man 81
Friend 40	The orator 82
Into a new day 41	It's all about me 83
Jealousy 42	Trees 84
	Epilogue 85

Dictionary of Maori words:

Whare-House/Home
Ka Pai-All good
Aroha Nui-Big love
Pai Kare-Good friend
Hori-Slang for a Maori male

BAD NEWS IS GOOD NEWS

good news is bad news isn't this true
earthquakes, hurricanes, murders, famine, debt, who's who
why don't we try peace, love and faith in the one above
He's not just above, He's you, me, the creek, the sea, the bee
it's not them or we, it's us, let's not fuss anymore we all know the score
there's ample around, can we count the raindrops and its sounds
infinity everywhere there's nothing really to fear but fear itself
let's stop being selfish cause we'll be left on the shelf
i would take on this place called hell
fight my hardest to the bell
if He's to blame for the mess, the flame
but flame is revered in places, the heart for one
so how many angels can we look at
even one
good news is bad news, bad news is good
let's change the scene, get someone good like robin hood
or jack and the magic bean
steal from the rich and giants of this world
we're all in it together, we're tied to the weather
got no one else to blame for this severe cold and wild flame
yet we're stubborn, tied to money and won't change
there's infinite things up or down
let's see the good side drop the frown
let's clean it up for the next little things
and see what brilliance they can bring
i see good things for this iPad generation
maybe i'm wrong but why not create creation
lots of ways to go doesn't have to be all bad news
it's just the people in power and their views

BITS

Babycakes has bits, ass and tits
i like to touch those bits every once in a while
it's just not fair her walking around in her underwear
though it makes me smile
its like she's learned Kung fu
when i try to get through
her hands are too fast
can't seem to get a grasp
of the bits and pieces, she just unleashes
with a flurry of defence
my moves aren't quick enough, they're worth a pence
all the while we're giggling and laughing, having fun
trying to get my sausage into the bun
not tonight it seems i'll have to go to extremes
i'll give up the fight, she's too quick tonight
off to bed with a bit of sorrow
but eager to see what's in store for tomorrow

DAUGHTER

patience my child, don't get wild
for i am mild
pain in my heart i feel for you
you were taken from me by society
the cruel ugly masses
it was with pain in my heart we had to part
i sought to seek a new road to carry the load
away from you and mum so you would not hurt
or be dragged through the dirt
they were on me like flies
their words their alibis
they were great in number
like a giant awake from slumber
mean hungry for blood
dragging my life through the mud
i had too leave you to keep you safe
to fight for my life in another place
it was my love for you that drove me away
and that love still burns every day
i must fight for my cause until i hear that applause
redemption and true freedom will rise high in the sky
that's where i must abide
so we can be side by side
and that's when we will be together until the end
so stay safe my sweet patience

DOCS & LEATHERS

Edited with Virginia Wall

strolling through the yard in my docs and leathers
this kind of gear is built for this weather
sheeting rain, howling wind sometimes mother nature just ain't kind
it's a mid eighties set in these classics that are hard to get
i'm proud of my docs leathers black tee shirt and jeans
represents some past hard core scenes
this is hard wearing gear that just won't wear, tear, brake or rip
built for wild weather hard looks that motorbike trip
see a concert all the greats, that was the scene
these days its outta date but i just don't care
this stuff is hard wearing built to last gear
it's a long way down the track but it's been a while
Gen Y that know value for money, class, and style
i feel like a teacher the music of our era
i could be a preacher
the feelings coming back i know it is
cause these were the day's fun, freedom revolution was the biz

EXPRESSION

express yourself be true
only you can be you
your originality will shine through
only you think and do the things you do
it could be your big break
don't be afraid to make a mistake
we all shine at some time
keep plugging away day to day
use your strong points look at Marley he smoked joints
take the lead good things you will breed
expression is free look at me i'm into poetry
anyone can be great
it's never too late
you can go far
pick up a guitar
do some art take part
in something great
express yourself don't wait
express love not hate
help each other shine
expression is like fine wine

FOREVER IS NEVER

i gave it all i gave all every bit of me
i guess it was the ultimate fall
but forever is never between you and me
this negative set has made me so sharp
clear and true won true friends through and through
where are we on this cosmic map
is this grain of sand an endless trap
in a teaspoon of dirt there's more life than people
who i find can hurt more than dirt
count the ways you can love the beauty below and above
the ants the crickets an eagle a dove
love for one another
or drawn down from above
the power of nature the power of thought
are there any more mysteries that can't be bought
forever is never if you get what i mean
cause never is forever they both can't be seen

GEAR

we all have gear and with your gear there is no fear
love burning, forever yearning
to seek out, beyond all reason
at anytime, in any season
with the one you're with or those who aren't there
your gear will never disappear
it's worth more than money
it's as sweet as honey
it will drive you on
long after the fear is gone
you can belong to a select few
who will always love you
that's all you need
that's your horse, your steed
anywhere that goes, you won't have woes
heaven knows the feeling grows
it's an inbuilt sensation, pure elation
across time, across the nation
of mother, brother, sister
hood of love, sent from above

HATERS

haters are just masturbators it's true
people with tunnel vision who don't have a clue
they hate themselves and they hate you too
can't change them it's clear all they do is pump fear
they can't enjoy a beer without giving an evil glare
in your direction thinking their game of fear is perfection
but they're looking in a mirror so blunt is their attack
reflected back up their spine gutless wonders you'll find
it's a pity they're everywhere pumping their hate and fear
the key to beating them is love and laughter
and knowing you'll be ahead of them for ever after
so that's the plot there all headed for the grave to rot
they'll look back at a wasted life when they hear the final bell
and then so ever gracefully flung into hell

IN THE STRANGEST PLACES

i hear a cricket call outside my wall
moonlight and soft music i hear down the hall
is that the beautiful sound of rain fall
outside i hear a bird's love call
the stars at night shining bright for us all
in the strangest places you'll find this feeling
a beautiful peace a strange kind of healing
love for everything
can send you reeling
a glow that will grow inside your heart of hearts
something you can keep that never parts
it's borrowed and shared in the strangest places
a god given gift you can see on faces
the birds the bees the mice have it too
it's a god given gift its eternal glue
it's happened to me it will happen to you
if you just see the beauty put to our view
our ears and senses this stuff's free there's no expenses
it can power you like fuel this stuff's so cool
borrow or share this energy all around
there's an endless supply to be found
in the strangest places

THE BOX

hooray Virginia says i've been waiting for days
there's a knock at the door must be my box
what's in the box is it a frock or socks or something special for me
just wait Babycakes you'll see it's something for me
adulation all round what can be in the box
it's not a frock it's not socks i can't wait too see what's in the box
she pulls it apart it's a shock to my heart
it's a single blow up bed yea yea i've got my single bed
i don't have to sleep with you on the double bed
instead i can sleep in the spare room
me and my single bed do you see cutie there's no more gloom
shock horror me thinks this really stinks
we've hit rocks i'm beginning to hate that box
she's jumping around like it's a new love she's found
her and her new bed just not good for my head
oh well i guess i can sleep like a starfish
on my double mattress
i guess i'll have to bend a bit
otherwise we will really split
Ginny darling when will we sleep again together
just do this that and the other and i'll get back to you lover
oh well at least it wasn't a double blow up bed
otherwise i'd really be in trouble lol!!!!

LOVE

love is the deepest river the highest mountain
a gentle spring a roaring fountain
love is the peaceful night the soaring eagle in flight
love is the courage not to fight
love is to love things inside and above
to love yourself first then to let it overflow and burst
to spread like fire growing higher and higher
love is strong it will guide you along
it doesn't look back at wrongs
i look in my lover's eyes and without surprise
i find without a word spoken a love unbroken
i think of my whanau and i just know
the strongest love will always grow
love just doesn't know wrong it just gets along
with people nature who cares if they wanna hate ya
that's the opposite you'll find keep that in mind
love is true through and through
it does not hide and it does abide in me

MONEY

why so many poor knocking on the world's door
keep your hands off my stack says jack
there's such a need yet so much greed
money the root of evil money the seed
god bless those who try and not those who stand by
yes indeed there is a need to feed and shelter the poor
is it such a chore think of your brother help one another
and you'll discover the wealth you can give
to help people live
life is a gift we all must lift as one
until the day we can all have fun under the sun or son as one
we can see this day i'm sure so we can
all stand pure when we share a little of our pay with those in need
it's not their fault they can't get at the vault
it's locked tight by those with might
they need a helping hand not for us to stand and look
you need love for one another love for your brother
where's it all gone we must don that cloak again
we can do it i'm sure just take a look at your brother's eyes and realise
we're all the same in the same game
there should be one goal as a whole
make that an agenda start sharing the wealth
and joy a little money can give
so people can live and love

NO GREATER NO LESSER

the fact is the one is the one he is serious but true
he's there when i'm happy he's there when i'm blue
i could go a billion years and never find someone more true
it's duality it's becoming it's me it's free
i say how did you know that he says son from you
i try so hard to help him he says son you've done enough
i say dad am i too weak he says son you're tough
i want what you want you don't have to be rough
this is the real deal the silent support that i need
someone with integrity honour and not greed
to the end he will go with me through any darkened door
any fire any snow storm rough sea or bad whore
one thing is true this guide is no bore
compassion true love faith hope to the core
no greater no lesser level playing field it's no game
cool heads a way of seeing things brought to light
we're the same why should we feel unhappy or even a hint of shame
when we know fully and securely we're not to blame
endless help on the magic phone has everyone got this
or am i on my own small team that's true less mistakes that too
all we want to do is be free help people it's easy
it's cheap to run as free as thought in this nothing can be sold or bought
it's quicker than light and that's saying something alright
today yesterday and tomorrow why on earth should we have sorrow
there's an uncertain air around about filling not only my mind
but those around us with doubt one thing's clear there's a lot of fear
when really we should smile and not shed one tear
no greater no lesser we should all drink the cup of good cheer

NOW YOU SEE IT NOW YOU DON'T

let me tell you a story about now you see it now you don't
it's happening to me through me and it ain't no joke
i've always loved the stars the moon drinks in bars fast cars
add fire wind and rain and i've got a story to tell again
about now you see it now you don't
i look up the moon was there
i look away look back to see it disappear
i put something down turn around
look back can't be found
forget for a while then see it back again makes me smile
it's a game we play the good voice and I
doesn't matter the object as long as i can see it with my eye
you would not believe what i've got you would not believe the plot
it's timeless you see can you make heads or tails of me
put the southern cross in the wrong hemisphere
even the best magician anywhere
would find that hard to beat
me and the good voice think it's pretty neat
playing with the stars the moon and sun Jesus Christ we're having lots of fun
and to make it rhyme don't you think it's sublime
oh don't mention time time itself
we've cracked that one we will keep that on the shelf
for everyone to see
music was easy i just happened to let it be
now it all belongs to me
it's simple you see the hardest quiz
think it is that's my biz
so that's the story of now you see it now you don't
even if i die tomorrow we've pulled a hell of a joke

RESPECT

is it not too late to see
that a woman caused me to be
is it not too late to find
that a woman can be so kind
is it not a fact that love is blind
yet we fail to see
all she loves is me
nurture and care
shelter from fear and despair
a mother's love will always be above
that of any other love
between one another
strongest tie without a lie
have respect for your mom
the strongest love will come
she knows you best
better than the rest
she gave you a sister she gave you a brother
so you can love and laugh with each other
she fed you kept you clean
she knows where you've been
sent you to school
taught you to be no fool
your mom there's no one more cool
so tell her today how much you love her in every way

ROLLING THUNDER

is it a blunder or did i roll like thunder
took a bit of sex
is it that complex
heaven in a handbag
or are they dressed in drag
mom upside down wow
guess i'll have to build a wall bricks mortar and a trowel
is thunder scary or is it just hammer down
this rain that follows enough to drown
am i a joker or the jack are they against me or have my back
war is war ya just don't find peace in that
mother nature it has its own rules
extremes are now let's be no fools
blame it on the ozone blame it on the one
what can we do i say just have fun
no where to run that's surely clear
death and rebirth it's all there
fire and rain who reaps the pain
has this been done before and we're doing it again
let's sing songs make fortunes and fame
damn you can't take it with you what a shame

SETS

well here's something about a stage
is it an extra overtime or a page
in a book that lots took a look at
well i'm up to bat
to hit a six been shown sticks
to urge or to jeer me on
sounds like once upon
you could call it a set like setting a net
or taking a bet
who's on stage and who's looking
is the book about life or cooking
a harmless world war three people peoples and me
Vikings Cowboys Indians and a tree
is it a mirror or a harp depending on what you see
with an axe that's sharp
smiles to say like we won
cook looking for a bun
or Easter Bunny or Santa Claus
whatever it is there's no applause
unless i make it so laugh to myself
set the net or let it go
people seeing not seeing hearing not hearing
let's face it we're all human beings
did it start from a word loudly heard
is it a battle for a wife or is it just life
it's a set that's kind of a bet
of life and death
grown and sown burnt and blown
signs and pines flip the set take a bet
good verses bad to make people feel glad or sad
or does anyone really care about the outcome or are
we all just playing dumb

SHADES OF LIGHT LYRICS

eternal night eternal day
when all the light and dark
come out to play
if love is in your heart
these two things
are an obvious part
of everyday in which you start
it's very dear so let's keep it clear
lose the fear that shouldn't be there
for love is just a gentle emotion
it shouldn't be an erratic complicated commotion
but just the really amorous devotion
of a beautiful dual magic potion
seek it hard and grab it fast
because it will last way past anything it's that vast
for love is true so when you find it
keep it grow it and please don't waste it
and you will have a heart full of song
to last your whole life long

TARGET

i've been targeted by laughter a target for insult
a target for revolt
what have i done i ask the son
to reap so much pain again and again
i don't want to complain
but it's day in day out
i can't find my way out
i love and laugh be gentle and kind
all the good things that belong to human kind
it doesn't matter where i am or where i've been
what state or country i'm in
it's everywhere it's literally in the air
it's good and bad at the same time
it's today yesterday tomorrow it's sublime

PROPHET

i'm a prophet without profit
doing the dirty work the masses shirk.
no pay day in sight tortured day and night
for the King of Kings who has given me all things
love thought time it can't be bought
render unto Caesar what is his money
i mean
give to the king things unseen
i'm blessed i know i am
he is holding me in the palm of his hand
he's a friend til the end amongst the confusion
fear and pain
he will pull you clear again and again
i may be down but there's only one way up
to drink from the cup of love peace redemption and glory
i might be a hori but i've lived the ultimate story
epic tale i just cannot fail
for i am his wheels his sail

THAT'S HOW I ROLL

it's a role in a roll it's rock and roll
it's blues hip hop even soul
it's movies news stars sun moon
it's drugs in a teaspoon
it's a roll my friend and that's a fact
it's beer on tap
should i rock this story or should i rap
is this roll beginning
or at an end
let's think on that
it can't be stopped like the world let's get off
it's fighting it's war it's soaps what a bore
it's the net it's sex can go on
it's so complex it's trees it's bees
it's birds the two legged kind
it's fish on a dish food and surely people
is this the real deal the church and the steeple
come on let's not play let's all have a say
it's a silent fight day and night
an unspoken war eating the apple to the core
believers disbelievers silence all that
if you want to know from me where it's at
it's a role in a roll like the earth planets and stars
to the simple things coffee or drinks in a bar
walking the dog driving a car that smile from a stranger
feeling safe feeling danger energies around moving in out around
it's a new era we've found information abound
education a laptop away help your enemy he will help you back
that my friends is the right track
why war when so many are poor

THE MACHINE

are we gonna let this conglomerate machine roll over us like dirt
this tangled mess of wires designed to hurt
who's driving this machine have you ever seen
i'll tell you what they know where you've been
make a financial mistake and your burnt at the stake
machines have no spirit only numbers it counts
and that my friends is what it's all about
i'm not a terrorist as such it wasn't i didn't know enough
i just know too much
back to the machine and how it gleams
surrounded by flowers underground or tall towers
eye scan to get in
scan your card we know where you've been
tailor made shopping to your taste
right down to shampoo and toothpaste
the machine knows how to cut costs
it carries on at your loss
jobs gone overseas even they work harder than bees
the best produce we have left to rot
so carries on the conglomerate
where it leads to i can see clear as day
it's the Big Bang Theory in reverse one day
i can say with a pure heart and conscience clear
me and pop toiled many a year
just now i hear the machines steel twist and rust
til finally it becomes dust
the birds animals will dance again
no numbers credit cards taxes to give them pain

THE START

i awoke one morning into a
hell of a day
all i could think of is i have
to get away
was up all night fearful with fright
voices echoed we're gonna kill
you alright
look around no one to be found
the voices loud again and again
we're gonna give you pain
imminent death was around
still no one to be found
all night long my head was a throng
of voices death and fear
panic set in had to get out of here
had to confront the source
looking back it was me of course
had to walk people stare and gawk
behind my back they talk
soon it becomes clear
it's everywhere
nowhere to run too many to face
i'm absolutely all over the place
feeling deranged not ready for
such a change
exposed in the day
with an overwhelming feeling i
need to pray
make my way to a chapel
using the last of my apple
fall to my knees
i beg you father i beg you please
put me at ease
tears stream down and hit
the ground
a man says friend you have to leave
i look at him for some reprieve
that's how it started and it
hasn't parted
the voices and people still
at me today
but now i'm a fortress strong
and no man can say i'm wrong
i just get along
with what i need to do
writing is healing and to some it's
appealing
i've come a long way can feel the
light inside me these days

THE SWORD

truth and love are my sword come in climb aboard
i can't lie straight faced i'm open to every place
who did this to me or am i just this way
sword has a double edge
with my heart and soul i must pledge
to keep my honour integrity intact
i don't lie and that's a fact
gotta plan to be a man
it's been said let's put the bullshit to bed
i'm pure fear a roaring fire wind rain love and pain
i can be your deepest love from above
thought and energy running through the door
makes no difference if you're rich or poor
i keep calm while you use fear
why can't you believe me when i'm everywhere
i don't wanna hurt but i don't like dirt
the cruel smirk the smug sarcasm the thorn in my back
the racism that's so out of date
the disgusting stuff you've put on my plate
i'm brutally honest and straight to the point
all you want for me is to end up in the joint
the sword is sharp it's my thought you see
honed by negativity thrown at me
it will defeat those all hidden agendas
cause in the true god i trust and all his splendour

WHAT'S IN THE MEDICATION

do you want to die
then give our medication a try
if things are tough it will help you get by
believe you me there's ample supply
be quick and give it a fly
it's subsidised by medicare
you can get it almost anywhere
so don't be slow be sure of a thrill
seems life threatening after you take a pill
but you can survive almost any old thing
any dark psychotic twisted emotion you can bring
our brilliant medication will make the bell ring
in our endless seeking battling road
you will never get bored with the load
but if you finally see it as we do
endless humor will be given to you
funny debate stay up until late
serious agendas from past hard core benders
fun you will have because you've had enough of pain
until your back in the loop to do it all again

WINGS

it's funny how a white feather can produce so much feeling
when the opposite is true to me, it's wings from above, to me it's healing
it's waterproof, it's light and it's strong, it lasts long after the body has gone
it's colour does not fade, it doesn't hide from light or shade
it's not a weapon, it's not a blade
it's an instrument of flight and to me there's nothing more right
finely crafted and bound tight
it's made to do something the human body can't do
and that's fly around the sky so blue
is it not true angels have wings
do they fight or flight, looks like both,
am i wrong or right, there's a thing about flight
ever been in a plane
think it's bad, you must be insane
i wish i could fly, how many songs about that
thought can fly through any storm, mountain, fire, wall or sea
thought, i'm told can just cause to be
how's that for flight, doing it day and night
full on non stop til you get to the top
what's at the top, a view of the bottom
do you feel better, clearer, i'll give you a guess
you're no greater, no less
what's it all about, a giveaway sign at a roundabout
an interchange at a train station
a distant location, a vacation, a destination, space travel, communication
it's all flight, how else are we going to get there
or are we all just going to disappear
which could be good in a different sphere
time travel believe me it's possible, i've done it, déjà vu' it's true
which means i'm forever and so are you
thank god for a feather, doesn't make me feel under the weather

ADDICTION

ice valium coffee heroine coca-cola cocaine
what's happening is the world insane
cigarettes sex marijuana are we gonna ever give our addiction up
what's up pup
cigarettes is mine with a little beer and wine
i think it's fine but am i blind
economies getting hammered weathers all askew
i smoke and drink to the point where i spew
people ask what's wrong with you
even the little voice inside
from which i cannot hide
clean up he will say a golden path i will lay
but i want my coffee i want my smoke
you can't blame the world's problems on me that's a joke
okay he will say
then think of yourself your daughter your family your friends
your health not to mention wealth
i know he's so right that little voice inside
love is his angle not pride
but it's so hard this addiction this affliction
35 years of constant smoking
am i joking
do i really want to get to the point
where i'm choking
a golden path he will lay if i just give my addiction away
i mean what can i say
other than i should start today
and maybe in my own little way
i can save the day
for one and for all thank-you Paul

BEEN AROUND

i've been around enough to know
joy from sorrow
steal from borrow yesterday from tomorrow
been around seen a lot those that have those that have not
them that give them that take
he who is real he who is fake
been around a few blocks taken a few knocks
seen them scream and shout what's it all about
seen lust seen disgust driven fast cars taken the bus
all in all is it from height we must fall
or do we glide on puffed up pride
pushing love aside
i've been around up and down country to town
and you know what i've found
it all

BIG TIME FRIENDS

because my thoughts are everywhere
i mean literally in the air
for everyone to collect
i've earned a certain respect
social consciousness with me the key
i can cause change and now it's not so strange
to hear my big time friends teaching me on radio and TV
i've always wondered what's strange about me
it's a fact i now see it's no secret to me
i'm in the south east i come from the north west
my mind is everywhere i am the best
i can name names
but in the end they're all the same
big time friends i said friends well that depends
if i'm left or right if i do nothing or if i fight
i can rape womanhood that's understood
would you if you could i didn't know you see
it was all fun to me
and love my best card something i will never discard
that's why i'm a secret
i like that that means i'll always keep it
show me the money

CHEERS

years of beers cheers big ears
the frown disappears
shirk the work
look to perk up a dull day
check out the chicks the bros and hoes
who's cooler than who who's got a clue after a few
try not to spew hitting it hard
trying not to get barred from the tub of lard
across the bar
or the bouncer who wants to spar
try not to drool be cool
as you watch the honey walk in
you ask where you been all my life
but she knows you have a wife
she plays the game out
it's your shout
thinking you're made and you just got paid
you lay your money down
your friends join in say how's it been with a grin
it's on again the endless scene
so drunk it's like a dream
lots of laughs of course
a think about a bet on a horse
double or quits it loses and gives you the shits
the honey leaves she's had her fill
another wasted night your cash all in the til

DRUNKEN SENSE

ruba dub dub then off to the pub
to make drunken sense with
my two pence
money over the bar ha ha ha
a drunken joke to any old bloke
a perve at the women who are leisurely swimming
in glasses of wine looking so fine
for a time
to make drunken sense of this
lavish expense
one after the other the beers go
down slowly but surely that
happy sound
cheers and beers all around in
that sleepy little town

DUMB DUMBER DUMBEST

aha i caught you out i knew you'd read this
you wonder who it's about
i'll give you a clue it's about me and you
again and again Mr or Mrs Insane
riding the same train again
to make the same mistake twice is not nice
to make it thrice is worse still more
than that you're just ill
and need a pill to chill

FINDING MIDDLE GROUND

is there no middle ground to be found
the lowest lows the highest highs
the deepest canyon the starlit skies
emotional roller coaster built to crash
endless pursuit of that elusive cash
the wanton lust for the woman with a bust
to seek fortune and fame
only to be laid blame
for things you can or cannot control
it's the mountain peak
or deepest hole
when you're down on your knees
begging please
or on the highest high
soaring through the sky
you wonder, is there middle ground to be found
when you come down
a sense of place instead of disgrace
or looking down with a frown
feeling boastful and proud a sense of winning
endless grinning
but to be middle centre of your universe
to abandon the curse of up and down

FRIEND

to my dearest friend i give you
my all to the end
for in you i know i can depend
come hell or high water
i know you'll protect me and my daughter
pai kare you are welcome in
my whare
for it and i belong to you
and everything i do i do
for you
you are my spirit my guide
you are always at my side
i have humbly come to know you
and will never throw you away
i will love you deeply until my dying day
on this i will pray in my own special way
each and every day
to be by your side gives me
a special sense of pride
that resides inside
aroha nui my dear friend
i hope to see your face in the end
for you are the son you are the one
amen

INTO A NEW DAY

i now let go
of things that hurt me so
redemption is here
i let go of fear
do you hear my triumphant voice
as i rejoice
into a new day
i will pray for my accusers
who are the losers
for the morning star shines for me
isn't it powerful and pretty
it's a bit like me
i've found love from above
like a snow white dove
i now love myself
i won't be left on the shelf
to myself i will be true
into the wild blue yonder
i will no longer ponder fear and hate
i will be my best mate
because it's never too late to contemplate
that inner loving voice
to which i rejoice
because i've found it's my choice
to boldly step into a new day
and pave the way
for celebration of the annihilation
of fear and hate
let me tell you it's never too late

JEALOUSY

jealousy that has no bounds in me that can't be found
i tell you true if you do well i'm happy through and through
there are those that are fake and make a huge mistake
to be envious and curious
they'll pull you down all over town
in the most deceitful way
just to say
i'm better than you or he hasn't got a clue
but a loving truthful heart will pull those ones apart
just by being true i see the difference easily do you
but it's a passionate game they'll try to lay the blame
in a web of lies and alibis
but they can't disguise
what is ultimately their demise

THE ORATOR

THE ORATOR

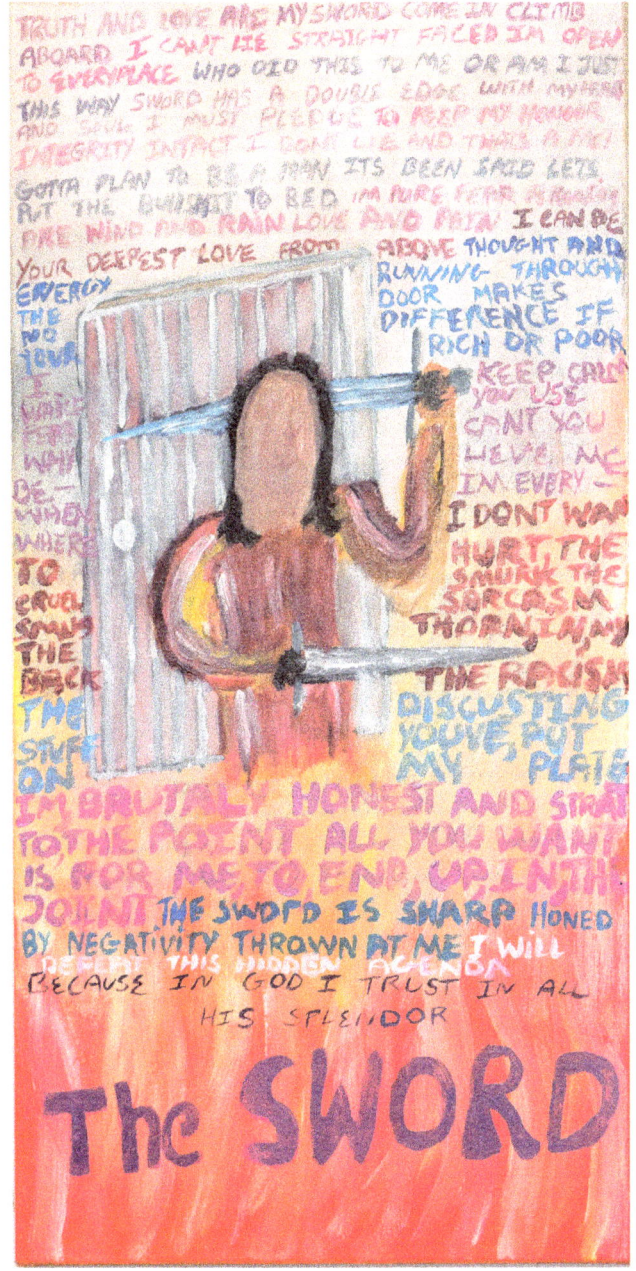

THE ORATOR

LOVERS EMBRACE

yearning bleak cloud shattered day
diamond lit eyes light years away
smouldering passion filled embrace
golden spirit beyond grace
take me sweep me fly me to that place
treasured in time
an opened fine wine
joyful tender lovers embrace once mine

LULLABY

blazing sun stroked time fades to shadowed closed blind night
long gone the bright bird song
enter stealth and black the grim reaper's cloak
enter lullaby tired eyes timely dreams to float
in satin laced sheet sleep we all must meet
time oh time the endless surge
enter lullaby for all for one
enter lullaby the going down of the sun.

LUST

i do lust
i lust for pretty faces
not them other places
although a bit of ass is
fine but not all the time
i lust love
love from above
love here love there
love from everywhere
a smile from a pretty face
has a little love in place
it's nice to see
because it's free
we should all collect
those pretty bits of love
like a wing on a dove
i lust i lust for love
with eyes that collect
receive and reflect
pure emotion
like an ocean
deep and full of life
you've got me flying
you've got me crying
i lust i lust for love

MAD

i'm mad that's sad i'm glad
you've been had
metamorphosis me ugly
but pretty
i'm a raging bull empty
but full
for i'm the one who answers
to none but the one
life is not fair but i don't care
i still love to share
i'm mad i've been told but
oh so bold
my soul can't be sold on that
i will never fold
but i'm mad or have you been had
i'm also resilient brilliant independent and strong
i don't need to be told where i belong
case in fact i'm fully intact
me and the voice in my head

MENTION

because i've had a shit load of attention
i know i'm up for a huge mention
in that special place in outer-space 36/18/6 and 7
you know that place i'm talking about heaven
i know what it's like embracing pure love from above
with eyes that see probably all that have passed in your family tree
because i'm well taught i'm a good teacher
you see it all comes to me in rhythmic poetry
the gift is permanent you see
given by the highest authority
i'm not a show off i just do what i do
i believe in myself and so should you
i'm not afraid to die because i know i'm not going to fry
in the fires of hell can't you tell
there is no hell
it's a stick to control have you worried about your soul
which leaves only heaven numbers 36/18/6 and 7
how about 9/10 and 11
their endless and so is heaven
and outer-space that's where i am in that place

OPEN BOOK

be controversial at the same time universal
be personal an open book say to your enemies come take a look
i've got nothing to hide
nothing to hide inside
it makes you a winner a non sinner
clean before God you may find that odd
that conclusion but deceit is an illusion
a confidence trick played by the slick
just know you can't lie try
it's not easy being this way
you can safely say
you've reached perfection
although you have no protection
there will be pain brought on by you
from the bad things you might still do
you'll have to learn temperament that comes with experiment
you'll find too much pride has to be put aside
you'll know when you win because it feels like you don't fit
in it feels like everybody knows where you've been
it's a long road but when you're done
the ultimate prize you have won

POVERTY

poverty and despair unfortunately it's everywhere
it's power brokers governments warmongers we fear
it's clear they have the power to right this wrong
in a world full of poverty politics and greed is where we all belong
the rich laugh as they lay their path
of destruction and wealth
money brings many things
like health cars boats and planes it is a God in its own right
the rest of us have to quarrel and fight
for a glimpse of light
did the true God give the few that right
to impose the plight of the masses
it's like molasses
a very sticky trap set by power brokers and all that crap
but we the many will not be denied
for one came one died
and through his name the world will realise
that a love so powerful cannot be denied

PRIDE

pride before a fall
it happens to us all
it's happened to you
it's happened to me
it's too late when you finally see
depth and despair
people who don't care
you were riding high
your aim the sky
taking no note of the passer by
you trod on toes hurt feelings
sent friends reeling
but oh how you stumbled
oh how you fell
now your world
is a definite hell
you should be cautious of what you say in a crowd
cautious of what you say out loud
for karma is always there
it'll turn on you any place anywhere
you used to laugh and taunt
but now you're spent and gaunt
oh pride oh pride those days are gone
i'm the toughest you used to say
i'll take on the world someday
fuck the world fuck the rest
i'm the best
now you're lying in a coffin your suit nicely pressed

SO BAD IT'S GOOD

check out under the hood
it's so bad it's good
spark plugs are new engine is old
sometimes won't start if it's too cold
tyres are worn broken grill
but i'm telling you this old unit will still give you a thrill
give it a push start comes alive with a rumble
this old baby's more than humble
paints faded but bumpers still shine
a couple of revs and this old unit's just fine
wait for her to warm up wind the squeaky windows down
this old classic is going to town
rumbling down the road she's a heavy load
off to do some shopping
exhaust pipe popping
roll up and park this old unit looks good in the dark
the upholstery still like new her heater works well and warms you through
she'll still take all your worries away with her hood down on a sunny day
so bad she's all good she'll make you smile
just check the oil once in a while

SPACESHIP

i saw it with my own eyes
with some surprise
three very large spaceships
cruising at a very slow clip
black edged in lights
triangular at night
the size of a football field each one
no noise no hum
it was the late eighties
i swear it's true, my maties
my good friend was there
we stared and stared
for ten minutes or so not a word spoken
the silence unbroken
my mind raced for a solution
only to be met with confusion
i remember thinking they were beautiful
probably dutiful
the stealth bomber of today
reminds me of these ships in some way
do they know something we don't know
that's proof we're not alone
where did they come from, where's their home
i'm excited and delighted we're not alone
do they traverse the universe
in their camouflaged giant ships
are they the universal police
looking for peace
my mind is at ease when i think of these
no harm was done to either one of us
it makes me think beyond life's strifes
and what lies ahead for humanity
to have witnessed this is a different sanity

WAR

fearsome time riddled spirit to visit once more
he ebbs and flows like waves upon a blood soaked shore
this untimely beast the unstoppable spirit of war
thou shalt risk all life all limb
thou shalt commit the ultimate sin
thou shalt rape pillage and plunder
thou shalt be loyal to the government we are under
thou shalt bring peace at any cost
why oh why is humanity so lost

WHAT'S WRONG

it's on like donkey kong
what is wrong
why is my life in every song
why do i feel i don't belong
why is this love so strong
yes it's on like donkey kong
i'm awake but i'm asleep
into my thoughts the masses creep
for who do i weep
for who do i seek
if not myself
then i am lost
to find salvation at any cost
so many clues
it's hard not to choose
you snooze you lose
what's right i ponder
well into the night
a range of emotion
a life of devotion
to love to laugh
is that too much to ask
what's wrong

YOU MAKE MY LIFE HELL

you make my life hell
when will the bell toll
you torture my soul
you butcher of meat
think you're pretty neat
sharpening your knife
to take my life
you attack in mass
i think you're crass
are you a leader
or just a beef and chicken bleeder
i've seen a lot since i've seen you
but your stigma sticks like glue
what is it with you
did the meat taint your brain
did it drive you insane
will we ever meet again
and will your friends be there
like they were before
on the butcher room floor
to torture me once more
alone i am, cause i'm a man
i stand tall in my belief
and i do get reprieve
from the big things on offer
cause i'm not a scoffer and puffed up
are you just a pawn in a game
am i the same
to me you're history
keep your new world butchery
cause that's what it is

BAD RAP

(it's about a bad situation)
man i've had the baddest rap ever
but what i get out of this
is something no one should miss
it's a lesson learned in time
it was forced on me so i made it mine
i do dudes see the shine
it's as clear as the sun and man i'm gonna have fun
big words don't give me that crap
cause bros i've had a bad rap
judge and jury without defence
kangaroo court with no support
but i'll beat this rap
and show you it was all just crap
shit fetishes upstairs
backward stares glances and fears
not me man i'm gonna be in the clear
i don't need your money, fancy cars expensive bars or flights to mars
it's all a load of fetish shit
and man you people don't know when to quit
look around check it out shit burning down in mass
this rap is just so crass
i have what's in my heart and that stuff won't part
and with that shine i'll be fine
i'll beat this rap and that's a fact

DARK GHOST

phantom shadow and dark ghost stay up late to make the most of a post
a kindred heart that will never part
a dual devotion that magic potion
from far away that's here to stay
eyes within eyes
thought within thought
aroha from afar
Kei te pai under one sky
never alone far from home
kotiro hells bells to the metal phantom shadow dark ghost
making the most of an early morn whanau from where we're born
hammering the haters see you laters to the masturbaters hello to aroha nui
that big all good hui
in the hokianga Mae
bring your koha
tena koto ka toa

DISHES

doing the dishes for the mrs is a good chore
doing dishes after a feed is a good deed
pots and pans plates too keep her happy
take my cue if it's a lot or if it's a few
come on guys it's not hard to do
check my verse
if you want to lighten her purse
knives and forks teaspoons and spoons
i guess you think it's loony tunes
put them all in the drying rack
believe me there's some payback
you will get to watch sport on tv
while you're served a nice cup of tea
doing dishes ain't so bad
in an apron with a scrubbing pad
the mrs will think he's a good lad
he ain't so bad
giving the pots a scrub
all the while your mind's on the pub
slip off for a couple after doing the dishes for the mrs
she won't mind after seeing your behind at the sink
it's okay darling you can go for a drink
i'll give you money honey
she will say get you out of my hair for the day lol !!!!!!!

DRUGS

meth ephedrine is a bad scene
better to stay clean
it will fry your brain
drive you insane sores on your face
have you acting out of place
fully addicted until you're caught and convicted
it takes over your life say goodbye to the children and wife
a good time you will have until you try to sleep
paranoia in your life will creep
a good time you will have but the down side is rough
it robs your brain of what little fun it has
never to come back you're nothing but a spazz
you've been had the rest is all bad
it's rife and it's for life
no one's been cured remember that when you suck on that point
you should have stuck to the natural and smoked a joint

FRIENDS IN A JAM

friends in a jam got the grand slam
locked in a social soup like a chicken coup
but there's friends to be had
through the good and the bad
locked doors
polished floors
medication
hesitation
elation
frustration
pretty nurses to make you smile
the wrong words you're in for a while
people who will help you
if you help yourself
flotsam and jetsam who've been left on the shelf
a reality that's real and lacks appeal
mania and depression suicidal aggression
talk is cheap but it's clear that's why some of us are here
a leap of faith that will take you to that place
where freedom lies beyond the disguise and alibis
of life's ups and downs smiles and frowns
warriors and clowns
it's a game we play night and day
staff and consumer serious humour
looking through the glass door
makes no difference if you're rich or poor
relaxation without taxation
everyone's got the answer that's why we're all here

HOLD

to be bold is to have hold
to face your enemies with stealth patience intelligence i'm told
to turn the other cheek does not mean you're weak
they will call you this and call you that
mostly behind your back
to get a reaction an ugly attraction
that leads to dissatisfaction
a situation you don't need
so this advice you must heed
hold be like a fortress strong
don't play along fall into their trap
you should know your own rap
so what they're doing is crap
just hold forget their ugly mugs they're just thugs
just hold strong and belong to truth and love
believe in yourself and the power above
and if you should fall and explode at times
be sure you know what your doing know it's a crime
and for crime you do time
one punch could end your life
it's like a double edged knife
jail or a hospital bed
like i say you could wind up dead
either way
so hold hold back don't attack
don't lose it all in an ugly brawl
i've seen it all before
seen so much waste in so much haste
to be placed on a fake pedestal
anguish is for fools
use hold intelligence love and truth as your tools
to combat situations caused by these fools
remember silence is golden don't use your fists just hold 'em

LADIES PLEASE

i'm feeling frisky a bit risky
show my fight do it right all night
by candle light see them stars sculling back at bars
when i'm in the room ladies there's no gloom
gonna take you there boom boom
when i step on the scene move over mr bean
i'm gonna be your dream gonna pull that shout
there ain't no dought gonna catch your eyes
like it's some surprise
gonna infiltrate baby make you wait
gonna make you sweat on the floor
like some whore
but you're too good for that
and baby that's a fact
take the a replace it with a u
it's gonna be me and you til the morning dew
gotta service the rest of the crew
so make it fast i swear this moment will last
over and done thank you hon

LONELY CROWD

in a crowd can be a lonely place
eyes darting from face to face,
looking for friendship without a trace
a love reaction with no satisfaction
feelings halt you want to bolt
the beer kicks in you ask where have you been
a quick glance your way
she doesn't want to say
you say have you heard
but you feel like a nerd
she's hot and knows what she's got
you're feeling left out
then she turns with a pout
what's the time sunshine
you flick your wrist this could be bliss
it's half past three do you wanna be with me
it's a bit late and i'm still waiting for my date
feelings hit the floor it's a lonely crowd once more
sexual tension put on suspension
glance around to spot a friend
looks like this night has come to an end
this lonely crowd has made me depend
on a beer in hand in this lonely land

MAN IN PLACE

we will fit him in without a trace
fulfil our wicked agenda
while we keep him on a bender
is it us or is it him, let's keep tags, see where he's been
let's make millions keep it a secret
schizophrenia a tag he can keep it
laugh at him using an extra sense
no matter what, no matter what expense
we will torture him with rock, numbers, old people and kids too
we will make him so puzzled he won't have a clue
we will say stand up, when he does we will knock him down
if he does anything good we will reply with a frown
if he gets a girlfriend we will call her a tart
if he says anything that makes sense we will call it a fart
just to see him die, our fetish bye bye
checkout no one, will cry the man in the sky
he's the man in the sky, did nothing wrong all along
few beers, bit of work, couple of bongs
a secret this big is evil and way out of control
he's now got the power to swing an election poll
is money his weakness cause he's still around, i hear
all he wants is a life and a beer
well i've got both didn't you hear

RESISTANCE IS FUTILE

Edited with Virginia Wall

(this is about love at its peak)
one hundred and forty four
thousand, we're
coming in
gonna clean up this great big
rubbish bin
full of sin
we're sick of watching this evil set
we're coming in you can bet
use wind and rain, fire and storm
your futile missiles be
tattered and torn
it's a disgusting mess that needs to
be addressed
he gave us free will
you've had your thrill
the world must take this bitter pill
on this grain of sand
on the palm of his hand
made with love and care
with everything there
he said subdue but you're
way of course
there's a hole up top,
things getting too hot, too cold
people being far too bold
it is what it is the story told
again and again
on this grain of sand or rice
whatever you want to call it
maybe ice

climate change all the clues
are coming
see it in the clouds the stars
the music bars
crickets humming
is it a trick
or is this set just too slick
and too quick to pick
let's not miss a trick
Put it together it's nature, money,
war, peace and weather
the later being the greater at this
time i'd hate to be a hater

ROLLING EAGLES

rolling through the city in my
tickford xr6
a bit over the limit, doing 66 clicks
watching the pretty chicks,
picking up tricks

got it in drive in this oversized bee-
hive of a city
looking at my girl that looks
so pretty
she's telling me how to drive, just to
keep us alive

on roads that are unforgiving
a fatal mistake is the difference
between dead and living

rolling to the bottle-o for a few take
home drinks
drink driving, man that stinks

keep it legal tegal
watch out for the rolling eagle
he'll slap a ticket on you in the
blink of an eye
electronic surveillance,
can't get away
even if you are sly

gotta keep that gold license clean
it means freedom in a city that can
be so mean
don't do anything stupid, only done
in a movie scene

but you can be a star in your
tickford xr6 car
you can go very far, get all
the jobs done
being clean on the road is a
lot more fun

go out tomorrow, do it all again
lose your license and you're in a
world of pain
nothing worse at a check point
blowing over the limit
shock horror, man i'm in it
knee deep in fines, no license
for a time
do the crime, do the time
pure and simple, it's sublime
don't do the crime, won't
do the time

not to be crammed in a bus
with people
who make a fuss
to be free in my xr6 doing
60-100 clicks
watching the road keeping my eye
out for the chicks

a gold license is a must
breaking the rules is a bust
my tickford xr6 and me is pure lust

RUBY ROCK CITY

Edited with Virginia Wall

(it's about my girlfriend)

i saw her at the R.E, so cute, small and sweet
i was sippin' on a schooner, just knew we had to meet
she rocked up to some friends of mutual acquaintance
i sculled that schooner, i'd run out of patience
i moved on over and slipped on in
it was time to make my move on this sweetheart and begin
i'd honed my moves for many years
i'll put them to the test over a few beers
wine was her choice
and she had such a pure soft voice
small and sweet this chic in this room you could not beat
some schooners, few wines later it was straight to the point
c'mon baby let's go back to my joint
shock horror, she gazed, she looked at me amazed
i'm not that kind of girl, dinner, a movie, a ring or a pearl
looks like my moves were at the bottom of a glass
turned me flat down, turned me around, kicked my ass
out the door
jaw hit the floor but a gem i did score
was her number- dinner's on the cards with a call
will make it real, it was her heart i wanted to steal
went to the R. E, to prep with some beers
the date was at eight
planned right, i'd be in heaven by eleven
she turned up what a sight, i was gone couldn't put up a fight
had to have this one way above, just had to be instant love
went better than i'd thought she said back to my pad
i can tell you now man, was i glad
so she turned out to be, the sweetest thing to me
ruby rock city

SENSORY OVERLOAD

the tv the radio smart-phone computer
buses trains cars planes
people bees pets wind rain trees
oh please, sensory overload my head is going to explode
the quiet and peaceful night
a pin drop can give you a fright
an urge too flight or fight
this endless overload day and night
dear god is there peace to be found
anywhere around up or down
this concrete jungle
angry people like sharp blades
in this mass masquerade
screaming kids all around
can be a deafening sound
but if you awake just before dawn
have a coffee have a yawn
there's a slight break you can't mistake
a beautiful peace an hour to release
from sensory overload in your own abode

SPACE JUNK

(this is about life)

god gave us a place with heaps of space
where we can grow heaps of dope to envelope and entwine a mega dope vine
bigger than the Rhine
where aliens and rockets abound
where no people to be paranoid about can be found
where no people even touch the ground
believe me you'll be blown away here looking at a certain sphere
poised between a gravitational pull
a case of darkness and of light
just put your space helmet on you'll be alright
this fantastic place with acres of dope
is in full view but you'll need a long rope ladder, stairs and such
because it's the moon you see
and man that's too much
what's the man in the moon saying or trying to teach
things this good are just plain out of reach lol!!!!!!

WHAT'S THE MEANING OF LIFE

get a job, get a wife
some good times, some strife
a load of money get your slice
an ambassador, a genius, a writer, singer, a cook
a teacher on the internet, a hero in a book
politician, what's your ambition, what's our condition
to help to take too true to fake
fruit salad, chocolate cake
ice cold, sun bake
catch a train, catch a plane, walk the walk, talk the talk,
and of course the magical stalk, with a baby new
could happen to anyone, has it happened to you
and what do you do are we all supposed to pair
have children and care, thanks for telling me so clear
before it happens and where
are you following me, me you, who's really got a clue
i see it all around, do you
or do you see it through me, cause when i see it it's free
because man it's huge, a section of sky, put to my eye
an ant, a dogs pant, lots of song can be right or wrong
i don't want to be in a fight, that's not it for me
fittest of the fittest it could be
but the meek will inherit, so what's it to be
good genes in jeans, right skin, lots of money
or are we all headed for the bin
isn't it funny

THE ORIGINAL

Edited with Virginia Wall

bang! sucked in the universe with a breath
thought can do that, life and death
angels full on, all around,
voices saying, we don't need air,
we can't be found
looks like it's on me, this timeless play
picking up the clues night and day
love's the top card
my guide tells me true
what's the rest of it, have to wade through
straight up the middle, that's the plan
grab the women and children first, save the honey and the pram
handbags easy, simple, fast
others watching think it's sleazy, guide says son told you it wouldn't be easy
what do you want son it's up to you, i want to save the lot Dad, what
would Jesus do?
just let it roll son, we'll see what happens, i'm with you
you've got the book let's have a look
this is fantastic like it's talking to me
love and beauty in everything i see
this is so cool, so sexy, so powerful, so free
dad what on earth is happening to me
these people treat me so cruel i can't figure it out
son i'm afraid it's jealousy, without a doubt

THINK ON THIS

Edited with Virginia Wall

(It's about thinking and other stuff)

you ask if i pray, well what can i say, all day all day
just thinking, is that how we really pray
or sit down and think about what we really should say
come humbly but true, that's cool, i do that too
but not much you'll find because to me he's ultra kind
given me gift upon gift, which one do i choose
humble but rich, would that be the ultimate cruise
gotta get there though, gotta learn to make dough
which in the end is bread and the yellow brick road
can i make it with what's in my head
they're gonna love me again i hope that can be said
when they know i love them anyway
is that just words or will it ever pay
think on this, is it a quiz or just my biz
it's something i've learned hard going for that ace of hearts
the best card of all, and the rest make the pack
i've played them all going down my track
it's money that brings, and the page i'm on is things
a big house, fancy car, luxury boat
what's the most eaten sheep or goat
who cares it's McDonald's, K-fried, big money
we all try
politicians cast your vote where told
might as well be an endless hole
broken promises, high flying benders
agendas that are paid for: that's cold

TUNNELLING IN

Edited with Virginia Wall

(It's about psychiatric dilemma)

tunnelling in bros
don't think it won't happen to you
slight negativity that builds and grows
tunnelling in the walls are real,
inside and out,
tunnelling in can happen to anyone without a doubt
it's the things you feel and say
tunnelling in can happen to you someday
and believe me when you get there inside and out,
you've reached a certain goal without a doubt
gold glimmers, tar, smoke abound
you've tunnelled in and that's what you've found
empty faces with shades of light,
the endless urge to fight or flight
but there's walls you see, you have to box
you've tunnelled in, you've hit the rocks
keep your socks clean, your t shirt and jeans
you've tunnelled in without a doubt,
spruce yourself up, go back out for another bout
you can call a win a loss, a loss a win,
depending on where you've been
there's drugs in here there's drugs out there
you've tunnelled in, you can bet
in or out that's what you get
so it's a u shaped tunnel that you have dug,
after a while its like a bug, or a drug
round and round you go, where it leads only you know
box hard when you're on the rope
use love and not dope
and there's a golden path, with love faith and hope

ZEN

yin and yang the master plan,
nothing is all light and nothing is all dark,
in the deepest black there is a spark
in the lightest light there is some dark
that's an Asian equation long before Christ was around
in other cultures it can be found
look at the sky at night it's black and white
stars become black holes a criminal a saint
zen yin and yang is easy to paint
it's simple and pure can become a cure
if you're dark search for the light i'm sure in everyone it's bright
you could use religion! Love, passion to bring it to light
it's not a fight i'm just saying hoping, and praying
my light will shine bright!!!!

THE POP UP MAN

the pop up man is a spirit in the flesh
he could be european, african, asian, or bangladesh
he is everywhere he can't disappear?
is he a friend or is he omega the end?
he's following me around i don't know why
what he tells me i do try,
is this temperamental friend the beginning and the end
i need to identify this man to figure out his plan
is he good or bad why do i feel so pressured so sad?

is my reward in heaven
the good voice calls me an eleven
he is a ten and he's been there since way back then
the good voice tells me the lot
the pop up man has another plot,
and doesn't talk a lot,
i don't like his plan for me it seems very unhealthy,
the pop up man is unhappy with me,
what did i do cut down his tree?
i've cracked time déjà vu', pop up man what else can you do?
i've moved sun, moon, stars, clouds,
lots of things! of what i can be proud,
pop up man i'm figuring you out,
confidence man with out a doubt
double meaning you could call it screening,
your time is near,
i will see you disappear

THE ORATOR

i awoke one day with a voice in my head
the orator who is not dead
and never will be you see
it's a confusing mess at times
but i know when it's him he's so kind
gentle truth and love the orator is sent from above
his message is clear love and truth to hold dear
there are other voices i hear
hell bent on destruction pain and fear
they battle for my soul in real life it takes its toll
weary tired and spent at times
until the orator hits me with some loving rhymes
my soul rejoices those are my choices
without a doubt i love the orator through time and space
he loves me back anywhere any place
that energy has power unlimited the other voices are sour and jealous
they surround my soul which is a palace
let the battle begin love and truth digs in
fear and hate pound on the palace wall
i begin to tire but the orator is quick pulls out a mirror with a flick
deflects their attack it's energy he sees
and they burn like trees in a brushfire

IT'S ALL ABOUT ME

The sun and moon
revolve around me
look and see
i tell you true
they actually do
when you're the centre of
the universe
even if it's a little perverse
you have all the keys
if you please
love sex
is that complex
war weather
is that better
stars moon
have i come too soon
is that a play on words
well i too procreate like birds
is religion a lie well this one is not
i've got the lot
i've gotta talk it up
you won't pup
i'm just a walking god
i don't find that odd
i'm the best at everything
there ever was
just because
cause to become
i've done that one
pray to me my following sheep
and in return i'll let you sleep
don't think i'm a creep

i don't come cheap
you want a sunny day
well you'll have to pay
want some water
well you just oughta
it's not an easy task
sometimes i get out of sync
fill rivers and dams to the brink
sometimes floods appear
but that's my fault i'll make
that clear
a bit too much sun
well it's up to me and i like that one
when all said and done
i'm god the only one lol

TREES

if you please i love my trees
so too the birds and bees
the oak the willow the apple
the plum the birch the red wood
the naked gum
they bring shelter from rain wind
and sun
in their glorious colourful array
the sound of nature creatures
animals birds do play
it will be a sorry day to have
this taken away
by the blind bureaucrats
in their money making hats
laying concrete and tar for rail and car
it is sad to see a living beautiful tree
cut down so readily
like rats the bureaucrats build their
walls of stone and steel giving
living space a cold cold feel that only a tree can replace

EPILOGUE

This is a rhythmic collection of poems written over several years while dealing with auditory voices not only in my head but around me kind of like watching a story unfold. I swear I've seen miracles only God could do working through me, this is my story...

www.ingramcontent.com/pod-product-compliance
Lightning Source LLC
Chambersburg PA
CBHW062103290426
44110CB00022B/2700